MORE PRAISE FOR GOING INTO TOWN

T0266646

"The *New Yorker* magazine cartoonist has a style [*Going into Town*] lets readers see New York thr

"Both a bird's-eye view of the city and a memoir o⸱   ⸱er of Chast—who is, in my mind, as intrinsically New ⸱⸱⸱⸱ ⸱, ⸱ay, Woody Allen or Carrie Bradshaw—in need of such a primer." —*Vogue, What to Read This Season*

"Charming and hilarious." —*Library Journal*

"Chast takes a tour of New York as only she can. Her illustrations and photographs punctuate her hilarious, terribly interesting presentation of her city." —*San Francisco Chronicle*

"Sharply observant of the quotidian, perfectly capturing the idiocy and indignities we all suffer . . . We see a rare side of Chast as she shares her sense of joy about the place in the world she loves the most: Manhattan." —*Washington Independent Review of Books*

"It will make you laugh in that bittersweet way . . . Like a visit to the Big Apple, without the subway delays." —*Library Journal*, Barbara Hoffert's Nonfiction Picks for the Month, Editor's Picks of the Season

"Chast's voice and vision make this a singular love letter to a singular city." —*Kirkus Reviews* (starred review)

"Observations and advice . . . are mixed with the quirky character that oozes from the metropolis's every concrete pore. It's all delivered with obvious and knowing affection and captured with a keenly observant pen." —*Publishers Weekly* (starred review), Top Ten Comics and Graphic Novels of the Month

"A guide book full of wonder and optimism, a polar opposite of most current-affairs tomes about New York on the shelves today . . . Curmudgeonly but not the least bit cynical." —*The Bowery Boys*

"Chast makes everything that should be icky about New York somehow delightful . . . *Going into Town* is a total pleaser that could put a smile on just about anyone's face." —*BookReporter.com*

"I love this book as much as one can love a book without getting arrested." —Patricia Marx

"It's quirky and witty, her illustrations are as weird and poignant as always, and, most of all, it's just fun to see what grabs her attention. It will grabs yours, too, and change the way you view New York." —*The Philadelphia Inquirer*

Can't We Talk About Something More Pleasant?
What I Hate from A to Z
Theories of Everything
The Party, After You Left
Childproof
Mondo Boxo
Proof of Life on Earth
The Four Elements
Parallel Universes
Unscientific Americans

GOING INTO TOWN

A Love Letter to New York

Roz Chast

BLOOMSBURY PUBLISHING
NEW YORK • LONDON • OXFORD • NEW DELHI • SYDNEY

BLOOMSBURY PUBLISHING
Bloomsbury Publishing Inc.
1385 Broadway, New York, NY 10018, USA

BLOOMSBURY, BLOOMSBURY PUBLISHING, and the Diana logo are trademarks of
Bloomsbury Publishing Plc

First published in the United States 2017
This paperback edition published 2019

Bloomsbury Publishing Plc does not have any control over, or responsibility for, any third-party websites
referred to or in this book. All internet addresses given in this book were correct at the time of going to
press. The author and publisher regret any inconvenience caused if addresses have changed or sites have
ceased to exist, but can accept no responsibility for any such changes.

ISBN: HB: 978-1-62040-321-1; eBook: 978-1-63286-978-4; PB: 978-1-63286-977-7

Library of Congress Cataloging-in-Publication Data

Names: Chast, Roz, author.
Title: Going into town : a love letter to New York / Roz Chast.
Description: New York : Bloomsbury USA, An imprint of Bloomsbury Publishing Plc, 2017.
Identifiers: LCCN 2017044793| ISBN 9781620403211 (hardback) | ISBN 9781632869784 (ebook)
Subjects: LCSH: Manhattan (New York, N.Y.)—Caricatures and cartoons. | New York (N.Y.)—Caricatures
and cartoons. | American wit and humor, Pictorial.
Classification: LCC NC1429.C525 A4 2017 | DDC 741.5/69747/1—dc23 LC record available at
https://lccn.loc.gov/2017044793

4 6 8 10 9 7 5 3

Printed and bound in China by RR Donnelley Asia Printing Solutions Ltd

To find out more about our authors and books visit www.bloomsbury.com and sign up for our newsletters.

Bloomsbury books may be purchased for business or promotional use. For information on bulk purchases
please contact Macmillan Corporate and Premium Sales Department at specialmarkets@macmillan.com.

CONTENTS:

This is not a "definitive guide book" to Manhattan. In fact, it's not really a guide book. There's nothing in here about the Statue of Liberty, for example. Why? Because I've never been. I'd _like_ to go. Someday. Just not today. Please don't make me go today.

This is also definitely not one of those "insider's guides" where I tell you about the hippest clubs, the swankiest restaurants, the edgiest neighborhoods, the coolest gyms, or the store where the best people buy the most exclusive shoes.

It's not a history book. Do not imagine, even
for a second, that I'm going to tell you
a bunch of cool facts, like how Betsy
Ross invented concrete, or that a thousand
feet under Grand Central, somebody discovered
an old Pilgrim restaurant, and look,
    here's the menu:

It began as a small booklet
I made for my daughter before
she left her home in Suburbia to
attend college in Manhattan:

NINA'S
BASIC N.Y.C.
BOOK
FOCUSING ON THE BOROUGH OF
Manhattan

BUT FIRST, A LITTLE BACKGROUND:

When our son was almost three and I was pregnant with our second child, my husband, our son, and I left Brooklyn for a pretty, leafy suburb about an hour north of Manhattan.

There were five main reasons for this leap into The Unknown:

① This was 1990 - the middle of the crack epidemic. We'd had it with crime, the crack vials all over the sidewalk — all of it.

Mommy, what dat?

I eat dat.

② <u>free</u>, <u>excellent</u> public schools where we were going.

③ My parents lived in Brooklyn for some people, this would have been a plus, but I had "mixed feelings."

④ Sometimes, when you grow up in a place, you need to get away. I saw Brooklyn differently from people who came there from Wisconsin or wherever. Behind every cute organic food store, I saw the ghost of the sad, dark, odiferous grocerette of my childhood. There was nothing there for me.

⑤ But the main reason was this: we couldn't afford the space we needed. The four-bedroom house we bought in Suburbia cost less than a crappy two-bedroom walk-up in Brooklyn, even in 1990.

The decision to leave the city was

TERRIFYING.

I didn't know how to drive. I didn't like the idea of living directly on top of a boiler or a furnace or whatever the hell was in a house basement. I'd never lived in what my parents called "the country." Also, would we turn into philistines? ZOMBIES???

...REPUBLICANS???

But in 1990...

As our kids were growing up, I frequently took them into the city. I wanted them to share my love for my hometown. But about a week before my daughter left for college in Manhattan, I decided to check up on her sense of "logistics."

HERE'S WHAT HAPPENED:

Maybe she was yanking my chain. But on the off chance that her childhood in Prettyville, U.S.A., had truly stunted her block-understanding, I decided to make her a little booklet containing some basic stuff about Manhattan, where she would be living, at least for the first year. Something she could carry around in her back pocket. Some maps, some tips. Nothing too overwhelming.

Here you go.

Godspeed.

When I gave her that book, I had this hope: that if she had the right tools for getting around the city, and of course, some luck, because one always needs luck, especially in New York, she would fall in love with the city, the way I did when I was just a few years older than her. I wanted to introduce her to Manhattan and didn't want them to "get off on the wrong foot."

QUESTIONS ASKED BY
The Suburban Child

ANSWERS:

1. Gum (probably)
2. Fire escapes
3. I don't know, but let's keep walking.

·o·o O⟨══════⟩▷oo·

I feel about Manhattan the way I feel about a book, a TV series, a movie, a play, an artist, a song, a food, a _whatever_ that I love. I want to tell you about it so that maybe you will love it too. I'm not worried about it being "ruined" by too many people "discovering" it. Manhattan's been ruined since 1626, when Peter Minuit bought it from Native Americans for $ 24.00,

·o·o O⟨══════⟩▷oo·

Now my kids are grown-ups. The city has changed since I was 23. Things have happened. Some good, some bad, some very bad. But I still love it more than any place else, and hope you will too.

I'm walkin' heah.

2

BASIC LAYOUT

OF MANHATTAN

(I'm not kidding. You really need to know this.)

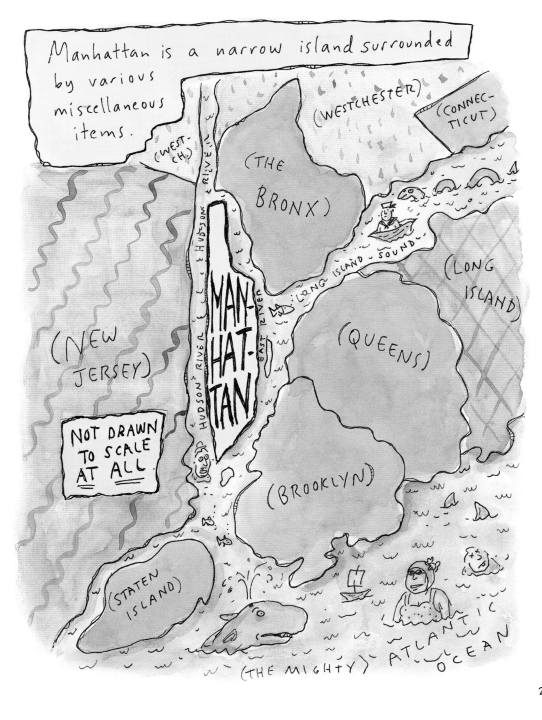

Nearly all of Manhattan is laid out on a grid:

FACTS:

- Avenues run NORTH – SOUTH.
- Streets run EAST – WEST.
- Broadway is the exception. It runs diagonally.
- Avenues are wider than streets, and the distance between avenues is wider than the distance between streets.

HOWEVER:

When you get below 14th Street, especially on the West Side, things get somewhat ungrid-like.

Another important fact:
Fifth Avenue divides the **EAST** **SIDE** from the **WEST SIDE**.

When looking for a street (not avenue)
address, the numbers start at ONE on
either side of Fifth Avenue, and increase
as you go further east or further west.

What this means is: 25 WEST 43rd Street
is a completely different building from
25 EAST 43rd Street.

25 WEST 43rd STREET

WEST 45th   EAST 45th
WEST   44th   EAST 44th
WEST 43rd STREET   EAST 43rd STREET
WEST 42nd   EAST 42nd
WEST 41ST   EAST 41ST

SIXTH AVENUE   FIFTH AVENUE   AVENUE   MADISON

25 EAST 43rd STREET

Also: Sixth Avenue and Avenue of the
Americas are the same thing. But no
one calls it "Avenue of the Americas,"
because GIVE ME A BREAK.

If the street numbers are going UP (21ST Street, 22nd Street, 23rd Street...) you're heading UPTOWN. ✱

If the street numbers are going DOWN, (21ST Street, 20th Street, 19th Street...) you're heading DOWNTOWN. ✱✱

✱ UPTOWN can also mean The Bronx.

✱✱ DOWNTOWN may mean Brooklyn. That's mainly when you're on the subway. ✱✱✱

✱✱✱ Don't worry about that now.

REMEMBER THAT OLD SONG?

The best thing about Manhattan's grid-like design is, you can't get too lost.

A term you're going to hear a lot is
CROSS - STREET.

For example:

Meet me at 678 Lexington.

What's the cross-street?

56th.

Perhaps you are wondering:

WHAT IS A CROSS-STREET?

A cross-street is simply the number of the street that intersects whatever avenue you're on.

The cross-street nearest to YOU is

76 th.

If all you have is an avenue address, find out the cross-street, or you're going to be wandering around like a lost Swedish tourist.

There are various formulas for working out the cross-street:

Just take the address...

Divide by six...

Find the square root...

Add either 17 or 52 or 93, depending on whether it's before or after noon...

But what year is this, 1978? No. Look it up on your phone.

find cross street 297 third av

Done.

The best way to get acquainted with the layout of the city is to **WALK AROUND**. To a great extent, everything in Manhattan is within walking distance of everything else. Between walking, biking, subways, buses, taxis, Uber-type apps, and everything else, who needs a stupid car?

WALKING AROUND

One of the greatest things you can do in life is walk around New York. Nature is great, but at a certain point, the mind wanders.

For some reason, I've always preferred cities to Nature. I am interested in the person-made. I like to watch and eavesdrop on people. And I really like DENSITY OF VISUAL INFORMATION.

Pick a random building in New York, examine it from top to bottom, and this is what you might see:

I don't know why that makes me happy to look at, but it does.

As I mentioned before, New York is one of the few places where having a car is more of a hindrance than an advantage. Walking is often the quickest and most interesting way to get around.

Also, in almost every other city, at least in the U.S., if you're in the downtown area in the middle of the afternoon, the streets will be <u>EMPTY</u>.

One of the reasons for that is that most U.S. cities are too <u>spread</u> <u>out</u>.

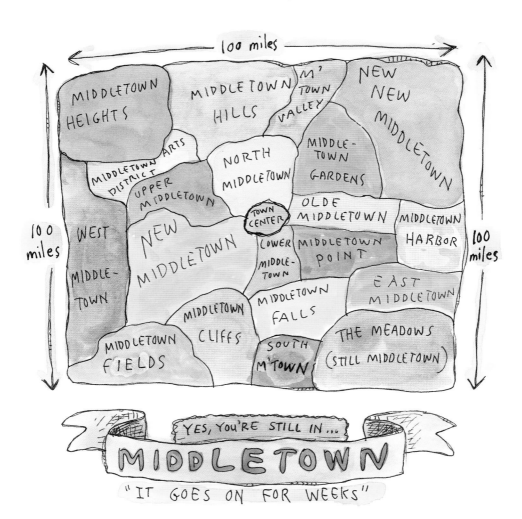

In Manhattan, especially in Midtown, the streets are rarely empty. The main drawback is getting stuck in a herd of out-of-towners who, for some reason, always seem reluctant to cross against the light.

45

At its widest, Manhattan is only 2.3 miles across. You could probably plug in a toaster in an apartment near the Hudson River, run the cord along 14th Street, and make yourself some toast near the East River.

Not that you'd want to do this. Just saying, if you did, it wouldn't be all that difficult.

If you are feeling antsy or out of sorts, pick a street and walk across it from coast to coast. Any street will do.

WEAR COMFORTABLE SHOES

The more nondescript your street is, the greater

MORE
RIBBON
UPSTAIRS

SALE

$3.99 yd

chance you have of making your own discoveries.

When you walk around, keep your eyes and ears open. Partly for safety - you don't want to get smashed by a bus - but also because there's <u>SO</u> <u>MUCH</u>

MATERIAL.

The people, the buildings, things expected, things unexpected, or something surprising you might find on the sidewalk right in front of you. Not money or dog poop or a dead body. Something <u>REALLY</u> surprising...

A couple of weeks ago, on a night of unseasonable warmth, I was walking around the city.

I was still getting used to the early darkness. Mostly I liked it. It made the day shorter.

YES! Almost time for bed.

The streets were crammed with people leaving work, students coming home from classes, tourists dragging suitcases, etc.

I like to look at people, but in the sly, indirect way that people look at other people in the city.

I was trained as a child growing up in the city to NEVER, EVER, look a stranger in the eye, because they could be a NUT!!!...

I look, I look away, I look at a building, another glance at a person, at a parking meter, at the ground, back at a person, etc.

My husband, who is from the Midwest, finds this peculiar.

People are nice!

Yeah, maybe....

Anyway, on this particular evening, as I was walking and looking and pretending not to look and looking away, something on the sidewalk caught my eye.

It was a large chef's knife, encased in a white cardboard protective sheath. It looked as if it had been newly purchased and accidentally dropped.

I picked it up and put it into my shoulder bag. "Not every day that one finds a chef's knife," I thought...

...AND THEN I COMPLETELY FORGOT ABOUT IT.

I hadn't been up there in thirty years. My daughter had NEVER been. And sometimes, it's actually fun to do a dumb touristy thing.

SECURITY

There certainly had been some changes since then.

SECURITY

Ma'am, do you have a **knife** in your bag?

Well, there's a teeny-tiny one on my Swiss army keychain...

Oh. Right.

THAT.

They believed me, but they confiscated
it and said I could reclaim it when
we came back down from the observation
deck. I never bothered.

Surprising things can happen at
any time.

Sometimes when you're walking around,
you decide you need to buy a lipstick
at an off-brand yet oddly compelling
store...

While you're walking around,
keep your eyes open for interesting storefronts...

... or objects ...

An installation by Hërd Banister-Klein, perhaps?

... or doorways.

Maybe one day
you will notice
the amazing
variety of
standpipes.

The more you
notice them...

the more
you will
see.

This one goes by
the name of
"Trixxxi."

← ▭

And this one is —
obviously—The God of
All Standpipes. Don't
get too close, and don't
make him angry.

▭ ⟶

PERHAPS YOU WILL NOTICE THE MANY...

STORES OF MYSTERY

Fred's Drugs

Surrounded by cut-rate drug- and cosmetic emporiums that sell, say, a bottle of XYZ shampoo for 79¢. Same bottle at Fred's? $2.09! How does he do it?

M & O Typewriter Supply

This place has been closed whenever one has walked by it. However, it's always there, meaning someone is continuing to pay rent on it. Why?

Beauty-Moi Frocks

Weird clothes, always five seasons out of date. Has been there forever. Store is usually pretty empty except for racks and racks of pantsuits and the like. Who shops here?

Tip-Top Goods

Boxes of saltines next to cartons of hair spray. Wigs, Christmas decorations, halter tops, institutional-sized jars of olives. Did all of this stuff "fall off a truck" or what?

OR THE ANCIENT LANDMARKS
OF NEW YORK CITY

Scaffold, West 81ST Street
Is believed to have originated in the early 12th century A.D.

Sidewalk Crater, Amsterdam Avenue
Has been there since the time of the Pharaohs.

Half-Deconstructed Town House, East 19th Street
References to it have been found in the Old Testament.

Abandoned Automobile, Riverside Drive
Fragments have been carbon-dated to the Jurassic period.

Walking is the best. But there are occasions
when it's too far to walk or time is short.
In that case, head for the nearest subway...

THE SUBWAY

The sidewalk in New York is like a thin shell covering a vast honeycomb of pipes and tunnels. The ground under which you are walking has been almost completely excavated. It is best if you don't think about this...

When I was little, my parents and I occasionally
took the subway from Newkirk Avenue in
Brooklyn into Manhattan - what they called
"going into town." These trips were for the sole
purpose of seeing a play - almost always a
musical, like Oklahoma or Man of La Mancha.

We'd go in, see the play, get back on the subway, and go home. We did not walk around and explore, or eat — either before or after the play — at a restaurant near the theater. My mother blamed her "bad feet," but I suspect there were other concerns:

There was only one restaurant they "trusted" to eat out in: a Chinese place one block from where we lived in Brooklyn.

Back in the day, one bought tokens to ride the subway.

One of my father's main pieces of advice to me was:

When you're going to the subway, ALWAYS HAVE A TOKEN IN YOUR HAND!

Because almost nothing is sadder than missing your train while you're fishing around for a token. He knew this.

Nowadays, of course, it's a Metrocard.

If you want to know New York, you <u>have</u> <u>to</u> <u>learn</u> the <u>subway</u> so get yourself one of these:

(It's helpful to know how the subway relates to the <u>layout</u>* of Manhattan.)

* See Chapter 2, Basic Layout

As I mentioned before, Manhattan
has an __EAST__ side and a __WEST__ side.

The (1),(2), and (3)
run - mostly - up
SEVENTH AVE. &
BROADWAY

The (2)&(3) are express.

The (1) is a local.
The (1) stops at every
stop.

The (2) &(3) stop at the
major cross-streets.

WEST SIDE

FIFTH AVE.

EAST SIDE

The (4),(5), and (6)
run - mostly -
up LEXINGTON AVE.

The (4) &(5) are express.

The (6) is a local.
The (6) stops at every stop.
The (4) &(5) stop at the
major cross-streets.

The (1),(2), and (3)
are your West Side
trains.

The (4),(5), and (6)
are your East Side
trains.

The letter trains are more complicated. They go up and down the length of Manhattan and also across. They do weird jig-jags. And, like the number trains, most of them meander into the other boroughs.

Gradually, all of this will make sense, except late at night, or on weekends, or when there's construction, when the trains can get a little "devil-may-care."

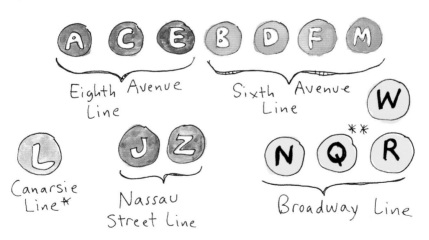

Eighth Avenue Line

Sixth Avenue Line

Canarsie Line*

Nassau Street Line

Broadway Line

(* Good for traversing 14th Street)

(** part of the new Second Av. subway line) (!!!!)

An important train to know about is the **SHUTTLE**.
The **SHUTTLE** goes on this route:

These two stations are very important because so many subway lines pass through them, which means that at those stations, you can _transfer_ from one line to another — i.e., switch to another line without paying an additional fare.

HOW DOES THIS WORK?

Imagine that you're on East 33rd Street, gazing at a pair of adorable socks. Suddenly, you remember that...

So, so cute!

...months ago, you agreed to meet someone you vaguely knew in high school for lunch on West 46th Street.

...and it's too late to cancel.

It's also too late to walk. So you go to the nearest subway — in this case, the one on Park Ave. South and 33rd.

Get on the **UPTOWN** ⑥ and get off at Grand Central.

Take the <u>SHUTTLE</u> to Times Square - 42nd Street.

Exit the station and run four blocks uptown like a bat out of hell to that godforsaken restaurant which is on, like, Tenth Avenue or some such, because now you're <u>REALLY</u> late.

BON APPETIT!

OUTTA MY WAY

The best thing to do is download a subway map onto your phone. In between cat videos, Instagram, learning Sanskrit, and bouts of Carton Crush⊙, you can study it.

And one last thing:

If the train is very crowded, and you see an empty car, don't think:

An empty car in the middle of a bunch of packed cars means that the air conditioning or heating is on the fritz; a nut is holding court; someone has had a pungent accident; or there's a dead person in there.

P.S.: TAXIS

Every so often, when one has procrastinated oneself into a corner, or one finds oneself in a remote area far from a subway line like Twelfth Avenue, or when one is schlepping something, or when one is simply exhausted and cannot take another step, one might want to hail a yellow cab. Here's some stuff you'll need to know:

> If the roof light (that thing with the numbers and letters) is **LIT**, the cab is empty.

> If the roof light is **NOT LIT**, that means that the taxi is occupied or the driver is off duty.

A.

B.

✻ HOW TO HAIL A CAB ✻

Step off curb facing traffic.

Raise arm ✱

Some people yell "**TAXI!!!**" or whistle. I do not.

Cab will pull over. Open the back door and get in. The end.

✱ Make sure you're not stealing someone else's cab. This is very bad form unless you are dying. It's also bad taxi karma   Cabs take cash or credit cards.

(Some people prefer to use Uber, Lyft, etc. I prefer the good old yellow cab, unless there are no cabs to be had. Maybe it's because of the instant-gratification factor. You need a cab, you hail a cab, you're in a cab.)

P. P. S. Don't neglect buses. These lumbering, oblong lane-hogs are slow as "molasses in January," and don't come for a long time, only to arrive in bunches. But sometimes, when you're not in a rush, they are a fun way to travel and see the sights above ground: the people, the stores, the mish-mosh of architectural styles. Try to get a window seat.

[Make sure you board the one that starts with "M" or you'll wind up in Queens or the Bronx or some other place that's not in Manhattan.]

5

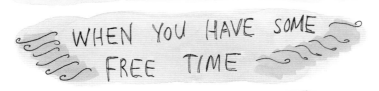

STUFF TO DO

WHEN YOU HAVE SOME FREE TIME

(AND HOPEFULLY, YOU HAVE A LITTLE)

One of the many things I love about
Manhattan is that you never really
have to face that existential dilemma
you might have to face if you lived in, say,
rural Nebraska :

If you feel that there's "nothing to do" while you're in Manhattan, then this is **DEFINITELY** not the book you should be reading. Also, you might be dead.

Day or night, any day of the week, any time of the year, including the dreaded wasteland of Christmas Day, you can find stuff to do. And it doesn't all cost big bucks.

Bye!

Museums and galleries are great places, if you like to look at stuff that other people made, and not all of them charge admission. The Met, for example, is a "pay what you want" museum.

HERE IS A ^{PARTIAL} LIST OF ^{ART} MUSEUMS:

- METROPOLITAN MUSEUM OF ART ("THE MET")

- MUSEUM OF MODERN ART ("MOMA")

- THE WHITNEY

- THE GUGGENHEIM

- THE FRICK

- THE RUBIN MUSEUM

- THE NEW MUSEUM

- THE AMERICAN FOLK ART MUSEUM

- MUSEUM OF THE CITY OF NEW YORK

- THE MORGAN LIBRARY AND MUSEUM

- THE JEWISH MUSEUM

- THE COOPER-HEWITT

The Met's permanent collection contains over two million "things": paintings and sculptures and costumes and snuff boxes and ceramic tiles and armor and all kinds of stuff from all over the world and from every era. If you are feeling low, it's possible that looking at a french tassel from the 18th century might cheer you up.

The great thing about the Met is that you can never see all of it. There is just too much. No matter how many times you go, you will always discover something great you've never seen before. And this doesn't even take into account the new exhibits that are always being mounted! In that way, the Met is like a microcosm of New York itself. There is a sense of the infinite. And you know that by the time you've seen everything (which is impossible, anyway) some of the old stuff will have vanished, and there will be new things to see.

You can immerse yourself in

Armorland!

The Met has armor from all over the world, not just the clanky metal kind. There's armor from Japan, China, the Philippines, Tibet, Turkey, Iran, and more.

Or you can look at old paintings and invent stories for them:

Oh, WISE MEN! forgive me for making your house levitate!!!

Perhaps you didn't mean to, but still: YOU MUST BE PUNISHED.

Heh, heh.

Oh, goody.

He's in for it now!

Plus, this is the third time. And everyone knows the rule of three.

94

Or, get fashion tips!
Next time you get your hair cut, ask for a
"Zazzera"- the "in" style in late 15th-century Venice.

But maybe the best thing
about the Met is that even at the
height of the tourist season – what
some people call "the holidays" –
when Manhattan can seem just
a tad too crowded, you can
always find a place to be...

ALONE.

Another amazing museum is the American
Museum of Natural History on Central Park
West and 79th Street. There are over 33 million
specimens here - plants, animals, fossils, gems, skeletons,
and lots more.
My favorite item on exhibit is the 34-ton
meteorite called Ahnighito.
It is SO **HEAVY** that it rests on supports
that go straight through the museum ALL THE
WAY DOWN TO THE BEDROCK OF MANHATTAN.
It is 4.5 billion years old - almost as old as the
Sun. Respect must be paid.

And remember: if you get museum'd out, it's not a class trip. You can leave whenever you want. There's lots of other stuff to do.

No...
more...
art...

Broadway play

Off-Broadway

Off-off-Broadway

Panel of alien abductees

Magic show

Modern dance

Comedy club

Didja ever eat an Oreo and...

Tragedy club

So, then I ate an Oreo, and...

Best hat on a dog contest

Opera

Ballet

Any kind of concert your "little heart" ♪ desires

Lecture by Gurdjieff devotee

A bazillion movies

Dive bar

I don' even feel these Moiler-bakers

The Strand ✳ (Open every night till 10:30 !)

✳ used bookstore

Gallery opening

...early Basquiat, late Hans Hoffman, seen through a post-modernist lens of...

Readings galore

This is my poem, "Hacken-sack."

And, of course, there's always shopping.
Not necessarily buying. Just... <u>SHOPPING</u>:

Don't forget to check out the New York Public Library on Fifth Avenue and 42nd Street, inside and out. The lions outside are named Patience and Fortitude.

The Circle Line is also great. This boat goes **ALL THE WAY** **AROUND MANHATTAN** = a trip that takes around 2½ hours.

STARTS AT PIER 83, WEST 42<u>nd</u> ST. AND 12<u>th</u> AVE.

BEST IN NON-CRAP WEATHER, DUH

The Staten Island Ferry is also fun. It leaves from the terminal at South Ferry and takes about half an hour. And it's free!

I'm King of the ferry!

I've never taken one of those horse-and-carriage rides through Central Park, though. The horses always look depressed.

Don't pick me... Don't pick me...

One more suggestion: visit Grand Central Terminal, on East 42nd Street and Park Avenue. It was built at the turn of the last century and almost demolished in a fit of "everything old is bad and everything new is great" in the mid-1960s.

This disaster was narrowly averted, thanks to the efforts of many far-sighted, influential New Yorkers, perhaps most notably Jacqueline Onassis, and in 1976, it was declared a National Historic Landmark.

Throughout most of my childhood and early adulthood — the 1970's and 1980s — GCT was a real skeevefest. Ugly billboards covered much of the original architecture, the restrooms were gross, and decades of grime had completely obscured the zodiac mural on the ceiling. But in the 1990s and 2000s, when the city had some money in its pockets again, it was renovated and restored to its original, breathtakingly lovely self. It's the first place I see when I come back to the city from Suburbia, and my favorite building in the city, for that reason — and also because it's a reminder that sometimes, the good guys win.

Honey, I'm home!

FLORA & FAUNA

6

If you are a fan of wide-open spaces, Manhattan is probably not the place for you. Even when you are outside, it feels like you are inside, possibly because there is not much of a view to the horizon, at least on ground level. This does not bother me. I think of it as "_cozy_."

Building, building, another building, water tower, DONE!

THERE ARE AT LEAST

70

PARKS HERE.

Here are my TOP FIVE:

NAME OF PARK	LOCATION	WHY IT'S GREAT
Bryant Park	Midtown, right behind the New York Public Library. Between 5th and 6th Avenues and 40th and 42nd Streets.	A big square of greenery occupying space that otherwise would contain yet another giant office building or luxury condo tower. I'm o.k. with that.
Fort Tryon Park	Way, way up at the top of Manhattan.	Beautiful, uncrowded, and home to the Cloisters, which houses an amazing collection of medieval art.
Riverside Park	Goes all along the Hudson River from 72nd Street up to 158th Street.	One word: WATERFRONT. Say hello to New Jersey, all the way over there.

NAME OF PARK	LOCATION	WHY IT'S GREAT
The High Line	The Lower West Side - Chelsea. Entrance is near the Whitney Museum — Gansevoort and Washington Streets, but there are multiple points of entry. It continues up to West 30th Street.	This is not a typical meadows-and-lawns park. It's an elevated walkway where you can walk and look at all kinds of plants and shrubs and trees and flowers, and building-scapes and people. It's surprisingly beautiful and satisfying, and its construction and existence is profoundly optimistic about people: that everyone - not just the "elite" - is in need of beauty and wonder.
Central Park	Central Park West to 5th Avenue, West 59th Street to 110th Street.	The CROWN JEWEL OF MANHATTAN...

116

Of all the parks in Manhattan, Central Park—which covers 6% of the borough's total acreage—is my favorite. It contains lots of Nature, but is no more "natural" than an arrangement of flowers from your neighborhood florist. It was designed specifically for the pleasure of the public—i.e., YOU—by Frederick Law Olmsted and Calvert Vaux, who won a park-design competition in 1858. Olmsted said that the park was "of great importance as the first real park made in this country—a democratic development of the highest significance."

OLMSTED   VAUX

THANK YOU

Central Park contains meadows, trees, paths, bridges, bodies of water, boats, a bandshell, playgrounds, ball fields, benches, lamp posts, dense areas of brambles, jumbles of rocks, turtles, a merry-go-round, a skating rink, statues, a castle, a zoo, restaurants, an incredible number of birds including flocks of escaped parakeets ~

I saw an open window, and *that was* all she *wrote!*

~ and much, MUCH, MUCH, MUCH MORE.

Central Park offers its visitors all of the benefits of a walk in Nature - fresh air, sky, trees, grass, space, etc. - with none of its drawbacks:

Without Central Park, Manhattan would be unlivable. It really would be a "concrete jungle."

However, the wonders of Nature are
not limited to the city's parks.

A SELECTION OF MANHATTAN WILDLIFE

Mice

Rats

Giant rats

Albino alligators
in sewers

Apartment
cats

Itsy dogs

Non-itsy dogs

Psycho pets

But the main wildlife in Manhattan is probably insects: cockroaches, bedbugs, silverfish, etc. I still remember the first time I saw a waterbug*. He was walking along 14th Street, just like any other pedestrian.

*A waterbug is like a cockroach who has been exposed to that gigantifying kind of radiation you see in old sci-fi movies.

In New York, bugs live inside more than they live outside.
If you have an *infestation*, don't panic.
Tell your super. He'll arrange for an
exterminator to come to your apartment.
Chances are, you'll need him to come more
than once. Maybe every month. Look!
You've made a new friend!

Bedbugs are even worse. Don't invite them
into your apartment by picking up that
cute, discarded, BEDBUG - COLONIZED
THROW PILLOW
you see on the street.

The most common **four**-legged animals you'll
see on the street are household pets. Mostly dogs.
Not cats, who tend to prefer sofas to sidewalks...

If Manhattan had an official tree, it would be this one:

If Manhattan had an official animal,
it would be the pigeon...

Speaking of pigeons, perhaps you're
feeling PECKISH...

FOOD

One of the most pleasant things about Manhattan, as opposed to say, Death Valley, is the unlikelihood that you will run out of food or water.

My father used to carry a little bit of food with him when he went into town—

a banana

a wax paper bag with a piece of honeycake in it

a plastic bag containing a stack of graham crackers

At some point, he'd announce to my mother:

Elizabeth, I feel like chewing on something.

And then out would come the honeycake or whatever. My mother **HATED** when he used that expression—"chewing on something" but he used it all the time anyway. There are worse things to fight about. Probably.

One thing neither of them _ever_ brought with them was **WATER**. That was because back in the Olden Days, people didn't need to **hydrate** themselves every fifteen minutes. Who knows why this was ?!? It's a medical mystery.

But don't feel as if you have to carry around your own personal roast chicken. Food is one thing Manhattan is not short of, from your ~monthly~rent = dinner (not including drinks) type places to the humblest sidewalk stand.

My default restaurant is the coffee shop, also sometimes called the diner. Why? Because if you stick to basics, like grilled cheese or eggs, YOU CANNOT GO TOO WRONG. Sure, a daredevil might order Sushi Enchiladas, but that doesn't mean **you** have to.

"Pheasant Under Glass"! Maybe I'll try that!

Many diners/coffee shops are open 24 hours a day, 7 days a week. You won't be the only person who needs some french toast at four A.M. And if you are, <u>nobody</u> <u>cares</u>.

In Manhattan, every food ethnicity, preference, above is represented. If you can't find what you

aversion, allergy, craving, fad, or combination of the
want to eat here, maybe you don't like food.

And for those days for whatever reason you can't or won't leave the apartment, and you can't or won't cook, there's always delivery.

A Starbucks Reverie

OVERHEARD IN THE FIELD

141

So: you've walked around. You've gone places and looked at stuff: parks, museums, people around you. Maybe you've had it, and you want to go back to wherever you came from. Be my guest.

But perhaps you've decided that this is where you need to live, come hell or high water...

8

APARTMENTS

One of the first noticeable things about Manhattan is that there are almost no private houses.

Um... What's a "private house"?

A "private house" is what mainland America calls a "house." It's the opposite of "apartment." In Brooklyn, where I grew up, kids asked each other:

Do you live in a **PRIVATE HOUSE** or in an **APARTMENT?**

When you first move here, you will experience several different kinds of apartments.

YOUR FIRST APARTMENT

No stove, no closets, no view— BUT I LOVE IT!!!

A FRIEND'S APARTMENT

A *little* nicer than mine.

ANOTHER FRIEND'S APARTMENT

A *little* worse than mine.

KID WITH A TRUST FUND'S APARTMENT

How do they afford this place?!?

KID-WITH-SKEEVY-BORDERLINE-SCARY-APARTMENT-AND-MAYBE-SOME-SORT-OF-DRUG-SITUATION-WHO-KNOWS

Well...see ya...'bye...

FIRST SERIOUSLY RICH PERSON'S APARTMENT

There's a Rembrandt etching in the bathroom.

There are pros and cons about apartment life.

When I was a kid, my mother used to keep a crutch handy, so when the horrible upstairs neighbors, who had clearly never lived in an apartment house before, started riding their horses or whatever they were doing, she could bang on the ceiling with it. It didn't always work.

BANG!
BANG!!
BANG!!!

Living in an apartment with people on both sides and above and below, is different from living in a house. Essentially, one does one's best not to be a jerk. Don't practice your saxophone after ten p.m. and I won't move my furniture around in the middle of the night.

AND WHEN ALL ELSE FAILS:

When you live in an apartment building, you have no control over who your neighbors might be. I didn't know this guy, but I'll never forget my glimpse of his apartment.

WHERE: My old building in the West 70s.
WHEN: Mid 1980s.
WHO: Building handyman; me.

Do you want to see something kind of weird?

O.K.!

He opened the door to an apartment stacked from floor to ceiling with newspapers.

There was a narrow path that snaked around...

I saw an arm from a chair peeking out.

It's a miracle the apartment hadn't collapsed into the apartment below.

What the—

Apparently, the guy had died a few days before... STANDING UP.

The greatest thing about living in an apartment house is that you have a SUPER. Theoretically, this means that you will never, ever have to deal with plumbing or electricity again.

Make friends with your super. By that, I don't mean take him out for lunch and tell him about all your personal problems. I mean treat him with great respect, and tip him as generously as your budget will allow, whenever he fixes something, and also at Christmastime.

Finding an apartment in Manhattan if you're not a zillionaire is not easy. But it's also not impossible. If you do want to live here, you will probably have to recalibrate your idea of what is affordable, and also make a compromise or two.

* York Avenue = extremely far eastern Manhattan. Practically in Europe.

WAYS TO FIND AN APARTMENT

- Online listings
- Newspaper
- Rental offices/broker (additional fee)
- Sign on lamp post
- Friend
- Nice doorman
- Obituaries
- Prayer
- Karma
- Hexes
- Magic secret apartment dance
- Shrine

If you really want to live in Manhattan, don't listen to naysayers. It will happen.

In 1949, E.B. White wrote one of the best books ever written about New York City called Here is New York. In it, he wrote that there were essentially three New Yorks:

First, there was the New York of the person who was born here, who "takes the city for granted and accepts its size and its turbulence as natural and inevitable." Secondly, there is the New York of the daily commuter who arrives for work every morning and leaves every evening for home in the Suburbs. You will almost never see this New Yorker wandering around aimlessly or sitting on a park bench. The commuter gives New York its "tidal restlessness."

Last of all is the New York of the person who was "born somewhere else and came to New York in quest of something."

I didn't come to New York from Akron or Mumbai, but from deep Brooklyn, right across the East River. I moved to Manhattan to save myself from the life I had very clearly pictured as my destiny: living in a grim little apartment down the hall from my parents and commuting every day to Manhattan to a hateful, soul-deadening job. I saw myself on the train: middle-aged, wearing beige support hose and a dirty beige trench coat and some sort of horrible "office garb," clinging to a subway pole and wondering why I was ever born.

In some ways, I identify with all three groups. But it's with the last group, the "seekers from elsewhere" with whom I most identify.

I will always feel gratitude and astonishment that Manhattan allowed me to make my home there. It's still the only place I've been where I feel, in some strange way, that I fit in. Or maybe, that it's the place where I least feel that I don't fit in.

New York is always changing. The New York of 2017 is different from the New York of 1983, and both of those versions are different from E.B. White's New York of 1949. I'm sure, in 2097, it will be something else again...

I try not to freak out every time a favorite restaurant or bookstore closes. I remind myself that life is change, and that life in New York is _definitely_ change, and that it's pointless to get overly sad because the place where you used to buy sketch pads is now a Jamba Juice.

I'm not nostalgic for the grittier, <u>Taxi Driver</u> incarnation of New York of the '70s and '80s. I don't miss the muggings, the shootings, the dog poop everywhere, not wanting to use the public restroom at Grand Central, the heroin, the graffiti (the "fuck you" kind, not the "cool" kind), AIDS, etc. I _do_ miss the cheaper rents.

New York is cleaner now, which is good, but also fancier. And I'm not such a big fan of fanciness.

The most profound change in New York happened on September 11th, 2001, when — out of NOWHERE — on a beautiful late-summer day, two jet planes flew into the twin towers of the World Trade Center.

In that instant, any illusion that we were somehow immune to the horrors that happen in so many other parts of the world vanished.

I thought it was the first time we — New Yorkers — had ever lost our sense of invulnerability, but I was mistaken. To quote E.B. White again — from Here is New York, written in the wake of World War II, in 1949:

"The city, for the first time in its long history, is destructible. A single flight of planes ... can quickly end this island fantasy, burn the towers, crumble the bridges, turn the underground passages into lethal chambers, cremate millions ... All dwellers in cities must live with the stubborn fact of annihilation, {but} New York has a certain clear priority. In the mind of whatever perverted dreamer might loose the lightning, New York must hold a steady, irresistible charm."

But New York came back. This is the best place in the world, an experiment, a melting pot, a fight to the death, an opera, a musical comedy, a tragedy, none of the above, all of the above. We're a target for seekers and dreamers and also nuts. We live here anyway.

This book is a sort-of guide and also a thank-you letter and a love letter to my home town and New Yorkers everywhere. You know who you are.